A TREATISE OF CIVIL POWER

Books by Geoffrey Hill

A
TREATISE

OF

Civil Power

GEOFFREY HILL

YALE UNIVERSITY PRESS   NEW HAVEN & LONDON

First published in the United States in 2007 by Yale University Press.
First published in the United Kingdom in 2007 by the Penguin Group.

Set in 11/14.25 pt Aldus by Rowland Phototypesetting Ltd., Bury St. Edmunds, Suffolk

Printed in the United States of America.

Library of Congress Control Number: 2007930943

ISBN 978-0-300-12617-4 (hardcover : alk. paper)
ISBN 978-0-300-13149-9 (pbk. : alk. paper)

A catalogue record for this book is available from the British Library.

The paper in this book meets the guidelines for permanence and durability of the Committee on Production Guidelines for Book Longevity of the Council on Library Resources.

10 9 8 7 6 5 4 3 2 1

to Ken Haynes

Justyce now is dede;
Trowth with a drowsy hede,
As hevy as the lede,
Is layd down to slepe,
And takith no kepe;
And Ryght is over the fallows
Gone to seke hallows,
With Reason together,
No man can tell whether.
No man wyll undertake
The first twayne to wake;
And the twayne last
Be withholde so fast
With mony, as men sayne,
They can not come agayne.

John Skelton

Acknowledgements

A word or phrase in italics mostly, though not invariably, indicates a direct quotation.

The fifteenth line of 'After Reading *Children of Albion* (1969)' is from a poem by John James.

Lines 7–8 of 'In Memoriam: Ernst Barlach' are from a letter by Barlach cited in Carl Dietrich Carls, *Ernst Barlach* (New York: Praeger, 1969), p. 55. Other quotations in this poem are from Kate Fletcher, *The Old Testament in the Dialect of the Black Country*, Part I, published by The Black Country Society, P. O. Box 71, Kingswinford, West Midlands DY6 9YN.

'On Reading *Crowds and Power*', section 2, is a paragraph from Elias Canetti's chapter on 'Fame', transposed, with slight changes of wording, into strophic form. I have used the English translation by Carol Stewart; the publisher is Continuum, New York. For Section 4 I have adopted the same method though with much greater freedom, or licence. My source is *The Sermons and Devotional Writings of Gerard Manley Hopkins*, ed. C. Devlin, SJ (London: Oxford University Press, 1959), p. 306 n. 196.5: editorial commentary.

'The Oath' is an imitation of Anne Hébert, 'Les Offensés', which is to be found in her collection *Le Jour n'a d'égal que la nuit* © Les Éditions du Boréal, Montréal. This imitation previously appeared in my *New & Collected Poems 1952–1992* (Boston: Houghton Mifflin Company, 1994).

In 2005 I published with the Clutag Press (Thame) a substantial booklet with the title *A Treatise of Civil Power*. Several of the poems in that collection are reprinted here, though at times in altered form. Clutag Press has kindly allowed me to retain the format of the original cover and title page. Some of the poems have also appeared in *Poetry* (Chicago).

Contents

The Minor Prophets

Joel in particular; between the Porch
and the Altar – something about dancing
or not dancing. No, *weeping*; but in the Bible
there's so much about dance; often of ill omen;
the threats of scorched earth and someone who resembles
the Scorpion King. They should film Joel:
A fire devoureth before them; and behind
them a flame burneth.

Citations I

This not quite knowing what the earth requires:
earthiness, earthliness, or things ethereal;
whether spiritus mundi notices bad faith
or if it cares; defraudings at the source,
the bare usury of the species. In the end
one is as broken as the vows and tatters,
petitions with blood on them, the charred prayers
spiralling godwards on intense thermals.

No decent modicum, agreed. I'd claim
the actual is at once cruder and finer,
without fuss carrying its own weight. Still
I think of poetry as it was said
of Alanbrooke's war diary: a work done
to gain, or regain, *possession of himself*,
as *a means of survival* and, in that sense,
a mode of moral life.

Citations II

Whether power rides on arias or recitatives
is not entirely an idle question.
Recitatives mainly I'd say although
people keep asking why your lyric mojo
atrophied at around ninety. I'd
swear myself blind atrophy's not the word
but that invention reinvents itself
every so often in the line of death.

Or if not why not: call writing nothing
but self-indemnity for what is denied it?
Yes, to be blunt, the pitiless wrench between
truth and metre, though you can scarcely hear this.
For yes read possibly. The train's just stopped
at the Jewellery Quarter. Perhaps if I alighted
I too would stroll a city of emerald
or at least zircon.

On Reading *Milton and the English Revolution*

I

The craft of vision is what I make of this.
They did so labour salvation, the dispossessed
their triumphal example. England
can do without most of us. For us
also language is a part-broken league.
Fix your own tail to the Jerusalem donkey.

II

Radiant urim; also the discreet
seraphic viscera. I say again it
can seem too much. The seeds of virtue
implanted by some mystical generation:
He that hath obtained to know this
goes without answer.

III

Wiped the old slur between liberty and licence.
Wisdom is back. How did it go, Wisdom?
The soul knows there no difference of sex.
Sympathy flows, utterance is end-stopped.
As if that stopped collusion. Perhaps it does.
Memory too returns, her key still in the lock.

IV

God himself is our Zion *where all creatures*
are fellow citizens: the ox with the butterfly,
the butchers in meaty aprons, Aaron's jewels,
a Commonwealth shilling from an oddments box;
great contrariety of mind; old reprobates
stuck with new-risen saints. Now cry *Amen*.

V
The mind closes or the imagination
turns itself down: if for no other cause
than play-catharsis. That being said
the choice should have fared better than R. Harris
with laryngitis. A simulacrum
of living speech strikes the aggrieved ear.

VI
Debridement that means reaming out the mock
virginity of the wound. Idiolect
that could be idiot dialect but isn't,
wrinching and spraining the text for clown-comedy
amid the pain, *the inward and irremediable
disposition of man* – this I can live with.

VII
The remnant is the redeemed. Forge the true key;
we shall insert as ordered, not *wrinching
and spraining* since I have strained myself.
How certainly words are at one with *all
corruptible things*. Bow down, bow down,
at the great stone altar sacred to billiards.

VIII
Getting into the act I ordain a *dishonoured
and discredited nation.*
Milton or Clarendon might well approve.
Can't say who else would. It smacks rather
of moral presumption. Things are not that bad.
H. Mirren's super.

IX

Everything is holy and we will reign
in our young bodies and make good our age.
O earth, earth, earth, Fairfield and Wribbenhall
shall resurrect like Cookham; Bagshot Heath
grow vines: for us – how else should I prophesy,
misguided, misconceiving, mis-inspired?

X

Joy is freewilling but – more – freeloading.
In the Book of Enoch, how the angels cover
all – is it all? – all the daughters of men.
I brood on this and am repelled by it
less than by my own gaffes of citation.
They have cut down our choice cedars. Curse for blessing.

XI

If God were not light – how does it go on?
Or at whose say so? Trouble the hypothesis
to be an immortal fact. It is enough
even mortalists concede the nub. *Save God's
being light, spirit could not have been.*
The marvellous webs are rimed with eternity.

XII

But to go out with all that ragged
history turmoiling in your wake,
a load of screw-wrath.
Regret cannot now get closer to target.
Sibylline interdict spells blunder – *resign!* –
though resignation itself proclaims the finder.

Holbein

I
The other Cromwell, that strange muse of Wyatt
and master of last things: it makes a fine
edge – wisdom so near miswielding power.
I think of the headsman balancing that
extraordinary axe for a long instant
without breaking the skin; then the engine
cuts its ascending outline on the air,
wharrs its velocity, dreadful, perhaps
merciful. And that moment of spreading
wide the arms as a signal. In fact it's all
signals. Pray, sirs, remember Cromwell's trim
wit on the scaffold, that saved Wyatt's neck;
the one blubbing – talk of the *quiet mind*! –
the other a scoundrel, yet this redeems him.

II
Imagine Hercules mated with the Hydra,
this king of bloody trunks their monster child.
More would have so rated him the arch
cleaver of women and old holy men.
Cerebral incest, his sperm a witch broth.
And Surrey, with his hierarchy of verse.
Meticulous the apportioning of time
in its reserve, Virgilian rectitude,
as though a full pavane of the elect
were the ten syllables to which they trod
as to the noblest music in the land,
lovely fecundity of barren heath,
Hillarby Bay, the Alde's thin-ribboned course;
sudden clouds harrowing the Anglian sky.

Parallel Lives

I

The Quyete of Mynde was a tough home assignment,
but you know that. The style seems to be made
with those like us, stranded and crying out
as brittle things in Virgil and Dante
that when you snag them flock the air with blood
making a mess of anger and lament:
the violent spendthrifts of their own hearts
to whom no quarter is given, no
quality of grace shown. The harpies have them.

II

The leathern wings belabour and I get
carried away. Plutarch writes of being
overdrawn by the affections. Quiet mind,
in Wyatt's English, is far from slumber
or waking lassitude. It is parsed here
because, since Wyatt wrote, that *continent
temper* which could play equivocation,
land it and slit it, find there the gold ring
of truth safe in its gut, is history.

Masques

Jonson also was excellent on work
within his mansions of erected wit.
For him it was defiance of the mob,
his adversaries mouthing at his call;
it was the shape of things held by the world
in various columns with the Latin scrolls
conspicuous like the Ralegh frontispiece.
I see Inigo Jones's great arches
in my mind's eye, his water-inky clouds,
the paraphernalia of a royal masque;
dung and detritus in the crazy streets,
the big coaches bellying in their skirts
pothole to pothole, and the men of fire,
the link-boys slouching and the rainy wind.

Harmonia Sacra

Harmonia sacra, a few sacred crumbs,
and we're a scared people. Not even now
sapped or snapped, the willing of the form
of nationhood, royalist, republican,
the seventeenth-century vision of harmony
that all gave voice to and that most betrayed.
This sounds like Herrick though without his grace.
I sing of times trans-shifting were his words.

On Reading *Blake: Prophet Against Empire*

I
Everything swings with the times. Cynicism
becomes innocence – such is my gash of thought.
Before you can say *Quid* or *Obtuse Angle*
or *Mrs Nanicantipot*, the milk tooth
hangs from the door-knob by its cotton thread.
Terror is opportune as is relief from terror.

II
This is where the cryptic opens. Blake
was afraid, shaken by the Law's dice-rattle;
but could have been an opportunist also
if luck had offered, or held, or just begun.
Coarser radicates nobler, by a kind
of sublime compromise with accident.

III
As to the sublime, don't take
my gloss on it. *The Spiritual Form
of Nelson Guiding Leviathan*: you behold
only the hero, the corpses, and the coils
of his victories, grandly weighed and spread.
For *a long age* you do not see the monster.

IV
The visual syntax so conducive to awe.
Which is why, in *Jerusalem*, he could
contradict and contain multitudes (I've
cribbed Whitman, you stickler – short of a phrase).
One poet is very like another and rejoices
in the final artifice. I mean great poets.

V

If *counting gold* is not *abundant living*
nothing else counts. That there are over-
flowing granaries of Imagination
stands neither here nor there. Money is fertile
and genius falls by the way. It doesn't –
but stays in its own room, growing confused

VI

as I suppose Will: Blake did, overwhelmed
by the spoiled harvest of *The Four Zoas*.

VII

At this end there is the mere amazement
for one's own dumbness and that of res publica
which do not correlate or even collide
except for public utilities, tyrants
of unaccountable error,
whose names are *Quid, Skofield*, and *Inflammable Gass*.

VIII

One dies dutifully, of fearful exhaustion,
or of *one's wrathful self*, self's baffle-plates
contrived with the dexterity of a lifetime.
Nobody listens or contradicts the screen;
though, homeward-bound, some find combustious
sights to be stepped aside from – an old body

IX

its mouth working.

To the Lord Protector Cromwell

1

1

Cut our loss. Make *Prognosticks* a back-list.

2

For labour of petty conundrums use

3

any commonplace book as model: strings

4

of synonyms, cramped maxims, anecdotes

5

nine-tenths botched in conveyance. *Turtle* is first

6

found in the Protectorate, meaning of course

7

the *sea-tortoise*; something having to do

8

with English sailors. England went maritime

9

and imperial; stared the world down;

10

rousing her own ire. Keep to this strong voice

11

like Milton's sonnet with its single purpose;

12
your known affect for Jewry and for music;

13
far-sighted blindness as the reach of vision;

14
like Burford's Levellers raked into their mounds.

2

1
Testudo is Butler. I note your strength enshelled

2
in that coarse-featured death mask, even so

3
better than a boiled skull, the mock of Tyburn.

4
How that exposed them, their French lisping,

5
their twenty-four fiddlers, the new theatre,

6
lascivious strolling and the royal whores.

7
But why history? Nothing appeals to it

8
except for murdered reporters: that's

9
not history, a folk-huddle more like,

(14)

10
with marathons and talk shows, brief Diana.

11
They made a film about you, that tough actor.

12
Guinness outplayed him as he finally

13
outplayed himself. Then there's the other thing,

14
Veronica Guerin's guilt-subliming wake.

3

1
Clue here is *Ireland,* not a conclusive one.

2
Below Times standard (old style). Dublin drug-heads

3
and Drogheda won't fit down or across.

4
Or if they will, then in a different warp.

5
Wanted: the well-judged end. You judged; were lost.

6
Luck of the common man at fifty-something.

7
Oblivion, self-oblivion, attend our needs.

8
It all goes on for ever. In that style

9
best known to himself, Milton pledged you immortal.

10
You made yourself with mortal stratagem:

11
the bowels of Christ, baubles, encumbrances,

12
with Ireton and the swaying major-generals,

13
the power-inducted saints and speculators.

14
You were above that, somewhere below God.

4

1
If the WORD be not with us, what is our

2
present legal position? I could answer

3
though possibly incorrectly. Say I would beg

4
out of this hire-house of ceaseless allusion.

5
I want out from this mire, say, of bluish flame.

(16)

6
Look up aphasia and aporia their origins.

7
The mystery of our being rests on such knowledge

8
if we're in neither of the sad sloughs.

9
I had a calling for England: that silver piece

10
I would pierce and hang at my neck, anyday.

11
There's an unfinished psalm doing the rounds

12
in the vicinity of my skull. My tongue

13
informs me this is not Hebrew but English

14
or Brobdingnagian | íf I may só construe it.

On Reading *Burke on Empire, Liberty, and Reform*

I
He was a realist in his providings:
the ways decency erodes and you
can see the slippage, though still ideas like *firm
and precise judgement* seem to possess balance
and even redemptive value. I'd say
outdone by the long haul (Wernher von Braun
essential American) not in the instance,

II
the predicate, of his first hope. Bromwich
is sound on this if the metre will take it.
He shows *participation*, of itself,
Idea's sacredness, the equivalent
communion of the just commoner, something
lived with, and in, to which he accords
the title of blessing. Burke was not

III
short of words, neither could he spare any:
the best description of the cogent style
I have yet encountered. *An avarice
of desolation* reawakes Tacitus.
Partial, impartial, unassailable
though many times assailed, like poetry –
The Pisan Cantos, The Confucian Odes.

IV
Culture is a dead word; let us re-
animate it. No, that would use
more resources than I have exhaustion
to yield, pledge, dig up, borrow against. *Strange
heterogeneous monsters*, an *impoverished
and defeated violence*. One scrawls obsessed.
Getting out of limbo is the earth-shaker.

A Cloud in Aquila

1

Get him out of there – Turing, out of
the *Turing Machine*. Some hope, if the rules
of immortality can be bent. I
should hope so.

2

The world of his prediction is not ours
as he conceived it. If there is innocence
it was as here: phase, segment; region
of Aquila

3

that validates and haunts first love, verifies
disappointment itself, *meaningless
in the absence of spirit*, whatever
the mechanism

4

of the thing, desire, the singing calculus;
impossible pseudo-science, Eddington,
McTaggart: their measure of the mind
nubilate, precise,

5

roving existence at call. Any way
the idea of love is what joins us thus far
though not past all question in the same
tissue of body;

6

and Morcom is dead now and Turing with him;
the Clock House demolished. At the sharp turn
where it was always dark the road steepens
to Housman's Pisgah.

In Framlingham Church

Surrey's ornate, unsatisfactory tomb,
not to the life at any rate, stiff
inaccurate pietas some seventy years delayed.
No point posing the card sonnet to Clere.
Nothing atones ever, but for a moment,
Holbein's unfinished sketch perhaps, as if
the sitter could not wait for the rich detail
that so delighted his proud port or span
when what proclaimed him was the wake of Troy.

De Necessitate

But that was Holbein's way not Surrey's whim
impetuous and impatient though he was:
the features finally rounded, trappings roughed
for later ornament, a word or two
to indicate style, colour – Henry's new men –
perjury, extortion – cut off at the neck,
a martyr here, or feckless victim; some
who would die safe in bed, some born to pass
into the shadow of the ragged stone.

After Reading *Children of Albion* (1969)

1

Time-expired accusation, a tendresse
of news-hounds, a cave of judges, a judgement
confounded, a covenant of fuddled sleep.
Children of Albion now old men and women
compromised by the deeds they signed in Eden
forsaking dearth.

2

Kemp's Jig was hard labour – London to Norwich.
I saw a man enact it for an hour
his stage about the space of a kitchenette.
Theatrical darkness, sound only, a hish,
a hisp, tissue of little bells. Then – bingo! –
lights! and a gold Albion uprearing,
electric with a static declamation,
a stance-prancer to his motionless fingers' ends.

3

The dancers, faces oblivious & grave, –
testing testing
the dancers face oblivion and the grave.

Integer Vitae

1

    Did you then say
circumscribed betrayal; did you say, the years,
the years alone have done this, circumambient,
did you so propose?

2

    The years will not
answer for what they have done, that much
is certain. There is no shaking them, we
might have foreseen this

3

    but refused.
No, refusal's too much said for such freedom.
What fails here is fail-safe, our modus
conjured by slide-rule.

4

    Ha! we can choose,
vivify what we catch from others' voices.
Thence to imperatives if you stall in
any manner of theme.

5

    Non-concurrent
the freedom and constraint outside of this
transient lock that is itself both
end and motive.

6
                    Juggling music
for piccolo and snare-drum, for any other
ad hoc hocketing of joy, always provided
there remains silence.

On Looking Through *50 Jahre im Bild: Bundesrepublik Deutschland*

It is not a matter of justice. Justice is in another world.
Or of injustice even; that is beside the point, or almost.
Nor even of the continuity of hirelings, the resourceful;
those who are obese – the excellent heads of hair –
the beautiful or plain wives, secretaries and translators.
The riots and demonstrations that now appear
like interludes, masques, or pageants, or students' rags;
the police water-cannon: you look for the film's director
but cannot find him. There is the captioned Wall;
there the Reichstag, the Brandenburger Tor
variously refurbished, with and without wire;
there's Willy Brandt kneeling at the Ghetto Memorial
on his visit to Warsaw, December of Nineteen Seventy:
I did what people do when words fail them.

A Précis or Memorandum of Civil Power

I
Could so have managed not to be flinging
down this challenge.
True way is homeless but the better gods
go with the house. *Cogito a bare
threshold,* as G. Marcel sagely declares,
of what's valid.
Come round to the idea, even so
belated, and knock. Echo the answer
in spare strophes that yield almost nothing
to the knowledge
outside them raw with late wisdom.
Quatuor pour la Fin du Temps not Gide's
doctrine of the moment which passes
as verity
in veritable suffusion. Grace
appears hardly spontaneous in that sense;
and in no sense whatever of the mere
veto or grab
of reality to our self-desires
as in a telling run of worldly luck
eminently worthy of these maimed lives.
I would forgo
this chant and others if I were not
more than a shade distressed. The sacrament
in its little hutch, the geyser's patio
of scalded earth,
beauty and disfigurement, all interest
set on the bias, accrued poverty
breaking every bank. The light exhaled
by spirits of *great
purity* is also in the finest painters

transfigured common light, *the crown*
of their achievements. Sage Marcel
withholds this gift
from artists of the word no doubt exactly
according to his lights which are quite something.
Knowledge, self-mastery, the self-embedded
body not ours
by deed of possession though suffering
possesses it and makes it ours in time.
I trust the arbiter – that's difficult.
My marginal
ontological reader, let her recoup
a line or two delivered without pathos.

II
I cannot work much closer to the slub
or perhaps it's
diffused like rumour, meaning diffused power.
How awkward this must sound. I'm reading Cornford
from a split paperback almost my age.
John Cornford dead
in Spain at twenty-one. Ninety this year.
Plaudits for Lenin and for Bela Kun.
Time turns sincerity to false witness
abetted by
our clear-headed stupidities; on occasion
a kind of brutishness conferred as love.
Heart of the heartless world he took from Marx
for a poem
part-way to timeless. Fine by either book.
The power-and-beauty mob has my bequest.

III
Not to skip detail, such as finches brisking
on stripped haw-bush;
the watered gold that February drains
out of the overcast; nomadic aconites
that in their trek recover beautifully
our sense of place,
the snowdrop fettled on its hinge, waxwings
becoming *sportif* in the grimy air.

IV
I accept, now, we make history; it's not some
abysmal power,
though making it kills us as we die to loss.
What lives is the arcane; by our decision
a lifetime's misdirection and a trophy
of some renown
or else nothing; the menagerie
of tinnitus crowding a deaf man's skull
has more to say. Woman's if you so rule.
It's gibberish
we bend to or are balked by on the spot,
treatise untreatised and the staring eyes.
The windflower has more stamina to fail,
the Lent lily,
the autumn crocus with its saffron fuse,
all that we fancy and make music of,
like Shakespeare's metaphors for governance,
nature itself
brought in to conserve polity; hives of gold
proclaim a gift few of us can afford.

V

Say everything works well but that it works
just like mischance.
Something of value is derived regardless
of our botched loves, uncalled-for, unconnived-at.
Civil power now smuggles more retractions
than hitherto;
public apology ad libs its charter,
well-misjudged villainy gets compensated.
I still can't tell you what that power is.
The statute books
suffer us here and there to lift a voice,
judge calls prosecutor to brief account,
juries may be stubborn to work good
like a brave child
standing its ground knowing it's in the right.
Letters to the editor can show wisdom.

VI

Well, there's a fortune in it if you sail
once round the world
faster than Jules Verne in his fantasy.
Fantasy makes a power of money too.
Money's not civil power in itself;
more the enforcer.
Types of physical prowess are a gift,
also computer-skills at a high pitch.
I lack the staying power of the grand
minimalist:
gnarl and burr, whoops of recycled basso,
the off-key sweetness of a single bell,
the world-wide reputation, decent life.
Let's all shore up
half-decent lives this Lent, *happy and holy.*
Two or three people I would call saints

without lust for sincerity which
Marcel describes,
*an exaltation [in one's] negative
powers*. I aim to cite correctly
but admit licence when the words won't match
with my own brief
to set this tricky artefact on line
for the realm of primal justice and accord.

VII
Why *Quatuor pour la Fin du Temps*, this has
nothing to do
surely with civil power? But it strikes chords
direct and angular: the terrible
unreadiness of France to hold her own:
nineteen forty
and what Marc Bloch entitled *Strange Defeat*;
prisoners, of whom Messiaen was one,
the unconventional quartet for which
the *Quatuor*
was fashioned as a thing beyond the time,
beyond the sick decorum of betrayal,
Pétain, Laval, the shabby prim hotels,
senility
fortified with spa waters. (When I said
grand minimalist I'd someone else in mind –
just to avoid confusion on that score.)
Strike up, augment,
irregular beauties contra the New Order.
Make do with cogent if austere finale.

G. F. Handel, Opus 6

Monumentality and *bidding*: words
neither yours nor mine, but like his music.
Stalwart and tender by turns, the fugues
and larghettos, staid, *bürgerlich*,
up to the wide gaunt leaps of invention.
Repetition of theme a reaffirming,
like figures in harmony with their right consorts,
with the world also, broadly understood;
each of itself a treatise of civil power,
every phrase instinct with deliberation
both upon power and towards civility.
At the rehearing always I think of you
and fancy: with what concordance I
would thus steadily regale and regard her,
though to speak truth you are ever in my mind;
such is eros, such philia, their composure
these arias, predetermined, of our choice.

An Emblem

Among the slag remonstrances of this land
memory reinterprets us, as with
a Heraclitean emblem. On a sudden,
sunslanting rain intensifies, the roses
twitch more rapidly, flights
of invisible wing-roots lift
from the lighter branches; a purple sky
ushering a rainbow. Now it is gone.

The Peacock at Alderton

Nothing to tell why I cannot write
in re Nobody; nobody to narrate this
latter acknowledgement: the self that counts
words to a line, accountable survivor
pain-wedged, pinioned in the cleft trunk,
less petty than a sprite, poisonous as Ariel
to Prospero's own knowledge. In my room
a vase of peacock feathers. I will attempt
to describe them, as if for evidence
on which a life depends. Except for the eyes
they are threadbare: the threads hanging
from some luminate tough weed in February.
But those eyes – like a Greek letter,
omega, fossiled in an Indian shawl;
like a shaved cross-section of living tissue,
the edge metallic blue, the core of jet,
the white of the eye in fact closer to beige,
the whole encircled with a black-fringed green.
The peacock roosts alone on a Scots pine
at the garden end, in blustery twilight
his fulgent cloak a gathering of the dark,
the maharajah-bird that scavenges
close by the stone-troughed, stone-terraced, stone-ensurfed
Suffolk shoreline; at times displays his scream.

In Memoriam: Gillian Rose

1

I have a question to ask for the form's sake:
how that small happy boy in the seaside
photographs became the unstable man,
hobbyist of his own rage, engrafting it
on a stock of compliance, of hurt women.
You do not need to answer the question
or challenge imposture.
Whatever the protocol I should still construe.

2

There is a kind of sanity that hates weddings
but bears an intelligence of grief
in its own kind. There are achievements
that carry failure on their back, blindness
not as in Brueghel, but unfathomably
far-seeing.

3

Recap on words like compassion that I
never chanced in your living presence;
as empathy and empowerment.
I did not blunder into your room with flowers.
Despite the correct moves, you would have wiped me
in the championship finals of dislike.

4
You might have responded to my question,
one will never know. You asked not to be
cheated of old age. No kidding, it is an
unlovely parley, although you
could have subdued it and set it to work,
met it without embracing. Edna
with her prosthetic jaw and nose
prevails over these exchanges.

5
Your anger against me might have been wrath
concerning the just city. Or poetry's
assumption of rule. Or its rôle
as wicked governor. This abdication
of self-censure indeed hauls it
within your long range of contempt,

6
unlike metaphysics which you had time for,
re-wedded to the city, a salutation
to Pallas, goddess of all polemics,
to Phocion's wife – who shall be nameless –
in Poussin's painting, gathering the disgraced
ashes of her husband. As you rightly said,
not some mere infinite love, a *finite act*
of political justice. Not many would see that.

7
If there's a healing of broken love it's not
as dyslexia's broken, learning to read signs.
In broken love you read the signs too late
although they are met with everywhere
like postcards of Manet and Monet, Van Gogh's shoes.
There are many rites exordinate to the occasion

8

though you have to choose one and get down to it –
it may involve grovelling or tearing of garments.
The just city is finally of some interest,
chiefly in the base senses of curiosity
and self-serving, if you understand me. You
do, of course, since I am using your three primers,

9

Mourning Becomes the Law, Love's Work, Paradiso:
a good legacy which you should be proud of
except that pride is forever irrelevant
where you are now. So it continues,
the work, lurching on broken springs
or having to be dug out or jump-started
or welded together out of two wrecks
or donated to a good cause, like to the homeless

10

in the city that is not just, has never
known justice, except sporadically:
Solon, Phocion – and they gave him hemlock
and burned his body in an unhallowed place.
And his ashes were taken up and smuggled
into his own home, and buried beneath the hearth.

11

A familiar rare type of resistance
heroine, like that woman, is required by justice.
Whether the omens are propitious or unpropitious
the Lysander takes off, heads south, the Maquis
line out the chosen ground, the landing-strip,
with their brave vulnerable fires.

12

Sometimes the Gestapo are waiting, sometimes not,
and she gets clear. But the odds are heavy.
The odds are heavy-set against us all
though medics call the chances symbiosis
in their brusque insolent manner that denies
self-knowledge as the sufferer, her formal agon:
that word you chose to use, a standard term
but not despicable in context of *Love's Work*.

13

Poetry's its own agon that *allows us*
to recognize devastation as the rift
between power and powerlessness. But when I
say poetry I mean something impossible
to be described, except by adding lines
to lines that are sufficient as themselves.

14

Di-dum endures formally; and the pre-Socratics.
Phocion rests in his lost burial place.
Devastated is Estuary; *devastation* remains
waste and shock. This ending is not the end,
more like the cleared spaces around St Paul's
and the gutted City after the fire-raid.
I find *love's work* a bleak ontology
to have to contemplate; it may be all we have.

Johannes Brahms, Opus 2

i
Oratory of those hammers: tenderness so defined.
Each phrase sounding its own future
resolution in opposition, discord in harmony

plus some other disporting of mastership.
Ponderable the élan and tensile bracing
with sorrow of acceptance

all-comporting; nothing that comes to grief.
Do not compound arrival with destiny
though here you could act so and be right.

Disposition of mind in the hands' posture.

ii
Or play off deportment into the found thing.
It will all go, the light clack of the keys
in the highest register, the incumbent sonorities

let us rehearse their passing, as Berkeley says
particles are units of the mind's energy:
in a while the body of our endurance

over and done with and still immortal
if we are that way inclined or otherwise
win cadence and closure.

In Memoriam: Aleksander Wat

O my brother, you have been well taken,
and by the writing hand most probably:
on photographs it looks to be the left,
the unlucky one. *Do nothing to revive me.*

Surrealism prescient of the real;
the unendurable to be assigned
no further, voice or no voice; funérailles,
songs of reft joy upon another planet.

Before Senility
dum possum volo

Intermezzo of sorts, something to do with gifts.
In plainer style, or sweeter, some figment
of gratitude and reconciliation
with the near things, with remnancy and love:

to measure the ownerless, worn, eighteenth-
century tombstones realigned like ashlar;
encompass the stark storm-severed head
of a sunflower blazing in mire of hail.

On Reading *The Essayes or Counsels, Civill and Morall*

1

So many had nothing; *we* have orchards
sometimes *ill-neighboured,* and are driven
to untimely harvest, simply to thwart thieves.
Our galleries may or may not be places
of seasonable resort.

2

Of Buildings and *Of Gardens* are themselves
exercises in prudence. *He that builds*
a fair house on an ill site doth commit
himself to prison. The sentences also
rise and fall.

3

There are *good whisperers* and *good magistrates*
by a noble collusion that is the style.
Even perjury and simony set forth
at a steady pace and arrive in time
for their host to receive them

4

with due courtesy and writs of attainder.
Of Prophecies is not beyond our scope
nor *Of Riches* our means. Is this Senecan?
Of the True Greatness of Kingdoms and Estates
is a major piece

5

whereas *Suspicion* is shortly dealt with.
What would men have? puts a radical question
as does the contest between wit and judgement.
Poverty is . . . tedious, and means chiefly
poverty of mind

6

that can accommodate what we would call
amplitude and quickness, which may be barren.
Religion, Matters of State, Great Persons
are to be spared jesting, *as is any case*
that deserves pity

7

though whether the dispossessed figure at all
is a question unasked at my lord's table.
There is much made of *precious ointment*
which is a potent magnanimity
that carries poison,

8

in my opinion, having read these things.
Dedications were tricky then; they're not now.
That's well worth an acknowledgement, a breather,
before the tide of *dark keeping*
sweeps us elsewhere

9

sputtering among the wreckage of late Demos.
So many had, and have, nothing; and Bacon
speaks of *privateness and retiring.* Consult
Of Judicature: the final book of Moses
is his landmark

10

and a good landmark, even: *the mislayer*
of a mere stone's to blame. So property
and equity are quits. My parents
never owned a house. It could be said
that was their folly.

11

The poor are bunglers: my people, whom I
nonetheless honour, who bought no landmark
other than their graves. I wish I could keep
Baconian counsel, wish I could keep resentment
out of my voice.

In Memoriam: Ernst Barlach

I should have known Low German; perhaps
the closest measure of it is Black Country
to which the Scriptures were transposed by Kate Fletcher.
All the children uv Israel blartid fer Moses.
This has something of you, the carvings and bronzes,
the peasantry of the lower Elbe your inspiration.
A powerful rough language appropriate
to everything human and untutored,
such as my great grandmother would have spoken.
Except that for you there were the Gothic woodcarvers
and a landscape of burning potato-haulms,
a flatland to get lost in if you had the will.
My heart bleeds with grief but you give me strength
you carved in Low German for an *Ehrenmal*
or *Mahnmal* on which the Mother of God
is rayed round by seven swords that have the appearance
of stabbing her in the back. The vertical one
we call *crucifix* without too much straining
of faith or credulity. But the Low German
snapped at an angle is a right bugger.
Min Hart I think I can read, but the squinching
obscures things. Anyhow the War did for it: Kiel
was ill-used. And independent peasantry
is a myth, and *Artist Against the Third Reich*
something of a misnomer. You tried to buy time
and to stave off calamity as I would have done;
you were not Haeften nor could I have been.
A thick clahd cuvvud the mahntin fer six days
and then another forty and Moses was stuck in it
and came out with his face glowing and folk *wuz frit on 'im.*
And *glowery* is a mighty word with two meanings
if you crave ambiguity in plain speaking
as I do.

On Reading *Crowds and Power*

1

Cloven, we are incorporate, our wounds
simple but mysterious. We have
some wherewithal to bide our time on earth.
Endurance is fantastic; ambulances
battling at intersections, the city
intolerably en fête. My reflexes
are words themselves rather than standard
flexures of civil power. In all of this
Cassiopeia's a blessing
as is steady Orion beloved of poets.
Quotidian natures ours for the time being
I do not know
how we should be absolved or what is fate.

2

Fame is not fastidious about the lips
which spread it. So long as there are mouths
to reiterate the one name it does not
matter whose they are.
The fact that to the seeker after fame
they are indistinguishable from each other
and are all counted as equal shows that this
passion has its origin in the experience
of crowd manipulation. Names collect
their own crowds. They are greedy, live their own
separate lives, hardly at all connected
with the real natures of the men who bear them.

(46)

3
But think on: that which is difficult
preserves democracy; you pay respect
to the intelligence of the citizen.
Basics are not condescension. Some
tyrants make great patrons. Let us observe
this and proceed. Certain directives
parody at your own risk. Tread lightly
with personal dignity and public image.
Safeguard the image of the common man.

4
As to the reprobate the rule is less
accommodating. God, it seems, does not
ordain them absolutely to damnation
though he forbears electing them 'in Christ'.
So, in the accomplishment of such decisions
as make or break us, there is no redemptive
ordinate will.

The Oath
After Anne Hébert, 'Les Offensés'

By order of hunger the starving stood in line
by dint of wrath the traitors were arraigned
by virtue of conscience the judges came to trial
by scale of offence the injured lay accused
by score of wounds the crucified made their mark
the forlorn hope the final wretchedness
the dumb possessed the barricades en masse
their speechless cry defiantly proclaimed
the Oath took arms against them street on street
its standards were the heavy rods of charge
in lieu of words the one word fire
blazed from its heart

Coda

1

Shredded – my kite – in the myriad-snagged
crabapple crown, the cane cross-piece flailing;
a dark wind visible even deep in the hedge.
I knew then how much my eros
was emptiness, thorn-fixed on desolation,
as rain rode up Severn and we, on high ground
eastward, scarped and broke it, like some beleaguered
folk of the Heptarchy.

2

If it's the brunt of years and luck turned savage
this is our last call, difficult coda
to the facility, the bane of speech,
a taint of richesse in the haggard seasons,
withdrawing a Welsh iron-puddler's portion, his
penny a week insurance cum burial fund,
cashing in pain itself, stark induration,
something saved for, brought home, stuck on the mantel,

3

industry's knack, say, of bright Whitby jet,
randomness added to, the Family Bible
its own inventory. Egregious Randolph Ash,
Possession – the film – excited me, the sex,
those marked-up brooches, sombre aery genius
ours at a price. *Insuperable jokes*
as someone far off said, hilariously.
The things that strike us can be patented.

4

I add – on oath (as prudent as you get) –
that the Welsh puddler's my great grandfather,
from near Newtown, brought to the Black Country,
his house on *Furnace Row* stands in the census.
This is as formal as a curse or cry,
the verse, I mean. Puddling's a way of life
and deadly in its kind, but more an art
than is some hammered threnos. Even so.

5

End that I saw how much is gift-entailed,
great grandson, and son, of defeated men,
in my childhood, that is. Even so I hope –
not believe, hope – our variously laboured
ways notwithstanding – we shall accountably
launch into death on a broad arc; our dark
abrupt spirit with fourth day constellations
that stood assembled to its first unknowing –

6

which is an abashed way invoking light,
the beatific vision, a species of heaven,
the presence of the first mover and all that,
great grandfather and Dante's *Paradiso*
understanding each other straight-on, to perfection.
I fear to wander in unbroken darkness
even with those I love. I know that sounds
a damn-fool thing to say.

Lyric Fragment

I hear an invisible
source of light skirling
off objects round about me – the granite portal,
women's hair also, and a deer's antlers.
In February a solitary oak leaf
dominates recognition. Are there
ancient coins wreathed with Medusa's head?

Nachwort

Somehow, with a near-helpless cry, I shall
wrench out of this. I don't much have
the patience, now, of the artificer
that so enthralls itself, impels
mass, energy, deep, the stubborn line,
the line that is that quickens to delay.

          – Urge to unmake
all wrought finalities, become a babbler
in the crowd's face –